# Supporting Children with ADHD

*Kate E. Spohrer*

The *Questions Publishing Company* Ltd
Birmingham
2002

The Questions Publishing Company Ltd
Leonard House, 321 Bradford Street, Digbeth, Birmingham B5 6ET

© The Questions Publishing Company Ltd 2002

Text and activity pages in this publication may be photocopied for use by the purchaser or in the purchasing institution only. Otherwise, all rights reserved and text may not be reprinted or reproduced or utilised in any form or by any electronic, mechanical or other means, now known or hereafter invented, including photocopying and recording, or in any information storage or retrieval system, without permission in writing from the publishers.

First published in 2002

ISBN: 1-84190-056-7

| | |
|---|---|
| Editorial team: | Amanda Greenley |
| | Linda Evans |
| Design team: | Ivan Morison |
| | James Davies |
| | John Minett |
| Cover photograph by: | Amanda Greenley at Hallmoor School |

With thanks to Sheila Thornton and the pupils at Hallmoor School in Birmingham for their kind permission to use the cover photograph.

Printed in the UK

## What is ADHD?

Attention Deficit Hyperactive Disorder (ADHD) is a medical diagnosis given to children who have developmental, behavioural and cognitive difficulties compared to their peers. It is diagnosed using criteria from either the International Classification of Diseases 10, or Diagnostic Statistical Manual IV.

ADHD has three components:

- Sustaining attention and concentration
- Controlling impulses
- Controlling motor activity

A diagnosis is only correctly made when there are problems in these areas over and above those found in the peer group and in more than one setting.

ADHD type behaviour is found in most people at some time, the factors changing such behaviour into ADHD are persistence, pervasiveness and intensity. It is thought that the root of the problem lies in the inability to inhibit behaviour. So for example we might have a fleeting thought 'I wonder what it would be like to jump out of this 14 storey window'. Before you know it an ADHD child could have tried this out!

A child born with an ADHD disposition will attract much negative feedback for his actions*. This is understandable because the adults around will have the child's safety in mind. They will also be concerned about social training and the constant effort required to keep the child safe, attended to, on task, etc can result in exhaustion for parents and carers. Very quickly the child begins to build up a negative self-image. This in itself is possibly the most damaging influence on a child's personal and social development. As professionals we should not apportion blame, we should increase our understanding and encourage pupils to adopt good habits.

Identification and diagnosis of ADHD is growing at an ever increasing rate. As teachers we need to look at this significant portion of the population (some estimates say around 5%) with increased understanding. This may mean that there is one pupil in every class who demonstrates this type of behaviour.

Some pupils diagnosed with ADHD will be offered drug therapy. The general consensus of opinion is that drug therapy should be offered as part of a multimodal treatment that includes some behavioural therapy as well. The commonly used drugs are Ritalin (Methylphenidate hydrochloride) and Dexedrine (Dextroamphetamine). Both are stimulants that increase the effect of neurotransmitters in the brain. It is the ineffectiveness of these neurotransmitters that is thought to be the cause of ADHD type behaviour.

*Throughout this book we refer to the ADHD child as male. This is for ease of reference only.

Use of the activities in this book can complement drug therapy. Medication should be used only to achieve respite from problem behaviours, and allow the child to get a feeling of life as it can be.

However drug therapy doesn't suit everyone. Currently, medication has to be taken every four or six hours, although this situation could soon be changing with new slow-release single-dose regimes. For the time being, we have a situation where Class A drugs have to be brought into schools and administered by staff. Some children do not like the feeling they get from the drug, or the stigma that sometimes gets attached to them by other pupils. There are also side effects including loss of appetite, sleeplessness, nervousness, anxiety, heightened emotions, exaggeration of existing tics, headaches and initial bruising. On the plus side, medication is reported by many to aid concentration, consequently schoolwork and social functioning improves and life becomes a lot happier for a child and his family.

The main section of this book contains activities and exercises for a pupil who has been diagnosed with ADHD, or whom you feel exhibits many of the characteristics of ADHD. It is ideally suited to a busy SENCo who wants appropriate materials to hand to learning support staff working one-to-one with a pupil, and the activities will support targets in an Individual Education Plan (IEP). In theory many of these exercises can be completed by the pupil independently. The major objective of the work is an increased understanding by the pupil of his own condition, and a consequent improvement in executive function. Teachers and support staff who work through this book with a pupil will increase their understanding of the types of activity a pupil needs to practice. These activities are not exhaustive or definitive, but are examples that can act as a springboard for your own ideas. Included are exercises taken from many disciplines, for example yoga, 'Brain Gym' and art therapy.

## What the teacher can do

As mentioned earlier, ADHD type behaviour occurs in most children from time to time. There is no ADHD behaviour that is so bizarre that a teacher will not have come up against it at some time. We are used to dealing with pupils going off task, seeking frequent attention and reassurance, and being impulsive. Use the following checklist to assess any pupils that you are concerned may have ADHD. If they achieve a low score this book will help. The problem with ADHD type pupils is that they will challenge even the best, most consistent and organised teacher, and they will do it relentlessly. Because of this we get tired of their behaviour and begin to lose sight of our good teaching methods. Many of the strategies mentioned in the following section will be ones that you have used many times before, but maybe you need to revisit some. The questionnaire on pages 4 and 5 is an attempt to help you to ask yourself candidly if you are considering these factors daily as you teach.

## Teacher's checklist

Use the checklist below to assess the pupil now, and again in six or nine months. Don't expect improvements quickly!

Agree a lot    1    2    3    4    Disagree a lot

| Date | | |
|---|---|---|
| Finds it hard to start work. | | |
| Finds it difficult to listen to other people for more than a minute. | | |
| Frequently loses his stuff. | | |
| Finds it hard to get any work finished. | | |
| Says things without thinking. | | |
| Does things without thinking. | | |
| Doesn't have many friends. | | |
| Daydreams. | | |
| Finds it really hard to sit still. | | |
| Forgets instructions just after he has been given them. | | |
| Anything going on in the room distracts him from his work. | | |
| Slow at getting ready for PE. | | |
| Interrupts other people's conversations. | | |
| Hates to wait. | | |
| Queues make him angry. | | |
| Gets frustrated and upset when he can't do his work quickly. | | |
| Likes to make friends but sometimes finds it difficult without help. | | |
| Friendships don't last. | | |
| Is sorry for things he's done wrong, then just does them again. | | |
| Talks incessantly. | | |
| Frequently out of his seat. | | |
| Interferes with other pupils and property. | | |
| Doesn't respond when concentrating on something he really enjoys. | | |
| Can concentrate hard on things he likes doing. | | |
| Asks lots of questions. | | |
| Likes individual sport better than team games. | | |
| Notices slight changes in the classroom. | | |
| Has lots of energy. | | |
| Has ideas that other people haven't thought of. | | |
| Likes to be the leader when playing team games. | | |
| Enjoys trying to solve problems. | | |

If the score is low this book should help.

## Teacher's questionnaire

Do I...

- make sure the child is looking at me before giving instructions?

- break down instructions into small chunks?

- provide prompts and signposts to help keep the child on task?

- create a bespoke behaviour programme that checks very frequently if negotiated targets have been achieved?

- ensure that precise behaviour-related positive comments are made four times as often as negative comments?

- provide a timer (kitchen, sand, etc) to aid completion of tasks in a specified time?

- ensure that opportunities arise for controlled movement around the classroom?

- ensure that opportunities arise for the child to take responsibility, e.g. to deliver notes, do errands?

- ensure that I have outlined clearly the behaviour that is expected of the children in my classroom?

- take curriculum time to explicitly teach behaviour?

- model appropriate behaviour at all times I am on view to my class?

- teach what type of voice to use in different situations and give feedback on practice sessions?

- consistently affirm the type of behaviour I want to see?

- always keep cool when the classroom temperature seems to be rising?

- get to know the pupils so that I am able to tap into their sense of humour?

- set realistically achievable amounts of homework?

- make sure I stick to routines in the classroom?

- check that my classroom is well organised?

- place pupils with ADHD type behaviour away from distractions?

- have a quiet place where an ADHD pupil can go to work quietly?

- negotiate with him when he needs to make the choice to go to that special place?

- have enough room in my classroom to seat pupils separately and to seat an ADHD pupil between two good role models?

- have a discrete negotiated signal that I can use to let the pupil know he is off task and it's time to get back on without letting the rest of the group know?

- know which tasks appear interesting to the pupil?

- always keep cool when faced with non-compliant behaviour, and calmly and slowly explain the choices available to the pupil?

- communicate that I am saddened by the non-compliant behaviour, but that I am not ruffled by it, and I will take time to consider my response?

- always state fairly the consequences of an action?

- encourage the pupil to consider the effects of his actions without asking him why he did something (a question he can never answer anyway)?

- target certain agreed behaviours rather than pay attention to every single misdemeanour?

- vigilantly praise appropriate behaviour?

- provide opportunities for a pupil to achieve in ways other than writing?

- discuss concentration and attention issues with the pupil, and ensure the pupil knows how to work on these behaviours?

## *Letter to the child*

Hello,

My name is Kate Spohrer. I am a teacher who works with children who have ADHD or concentration and attention difficulties. I have also lived with people who have ADHD, so I know some of the problems.

I hope that this book will help you to understand that you are not alone. There are loads of people like you, and there are lots of things you can do to make your life a little bit easier.

I hope you enjoy this book. When you have tried some of the things suggested in here, will you get in touch with me? I would love to hear from you. You can email me on spohrer@hotmail.com

Give it a try and get in touch!

Good luck,
Kate. E. Spohrer

## ADHD – What does this mean?

So, you have been identified as having Attention Deficit Hyperactive Disorder. What does this mean?

There are lots of different types of people. Some of those types are very slow and like to do the same thing over and over again, others like to do things quickly and like to do lots of different things. The picture below shows how most people are a bit of both.

But some people are right at the ends of the curve. You happen to be somewhere around here.

This needn't be a problem, but it could be if you don't get to know yourself and how *your* brain works.

If you are at the ADHD end of the curve you are likely to be easily distracted from anything you try to do. If you are like me you'll walk across the room to fetch something and return 30 seconds later having forgotten what you went for.

You could be a fidget, or hyperactive, especially when you are expected to listen to someone talking. You might keep changing position on your seat, sitting on your feet or lolling. This is all because you find it hard to keep awake in situations like that. You could be inattentive, maybe you like to doodle. I had to doodle through all my lectures at college. I thought of getting a pair of glasses with pictures of eyes on so I could go to sleep unnoticed!

You may be impulsive – that means you could say things you later wished you hadn't. Do you know that feeling?

You may not have all of these characteristics, or you may have some of them more in some situations than others. As I said, you need to know yourself, then you can work round your difficulties and use your strengths to best effect.

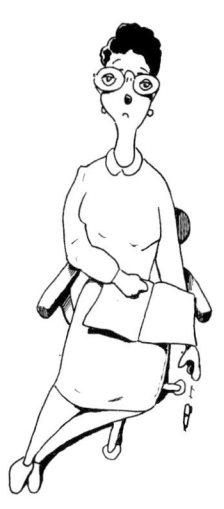

## Pupil's checklist

**Name:**

Look at the descriptions below and mark those things you think describe you.

SELF-ESTEEM

| Date | Agree a lot 1 | 2 | Disagree a lot 3 | 4 |
|---|---|---|---|---|
| It's hard for me to start my work. | | | | |
| I find it difficult to listen to other people for more than a minute. | | | | |
| I lose my stuff. | | | | |
| It's hard for me to get any work finished. | | | | |
| I say things without thinking. | | | | |
| I do things without thinking. | | | | |
| I don't have many friends. | | | | |
| When I should be concentrating on my work I think about other things. | | | | |
| I find it really hard to sit still. | | | | |
| I find that just after I have been given instructions I forget them. | | | | |
| Anything going on in the room takes my attention away from my work. | | | | |
| I am slow at getting ready for school. | | | | |
| I can't help butting in to other people's conversations. | | | | |
| I hate to wait. | | | | |
| Queues make me angry. | | | | |

Always hold on to this thought –

> THERE ARE A LOT OF THINGS I AM BETTER AT THAN LOTS OF OTHER PEOPLE.

**SELF-ESTEEM**

| | | | | |
|---|---|---|---|---|
| I get frustrated and upset when I can't do my work quickly. | | | | |
| I like to make friends but sometimes find it difficult without help. | | | | |
| I am sorry for things I've done wrong, but I do them again without thinking. | | | | |
| I can concentrate hard on things I like doing. | | | | |
| People think I can't hear properly when I'm concentrating on something I really enjoy doing. | | | | |
| I ask lots of questions. | | | | |
| I like individual sport better than team games. | | | | |
| I notice slight changes in my classroom. | | | | |
| I have lots of energy. | | | | |
| I have ideas that other people haven't thought of. | | | | |
| When I am playing team games I like to be the leader. | | | | |
| I enjoy trying to solve problems. | | | | |

Now that you have thought about these things you can plan how to help yourself.

## *About your brain*

Your brain controls your behaviour.

In the brain there are chemicals called neurotransmitters whose job it is to carry messages from one brain cell to another, just like a car or a bus carries passengers. Imagine if all the fuel in the filling stations dried up. We would not be able to get around. The neurotransmitters are like the cars and busses that move us around. In your brain's case it is messages that are moved.

What do you think would happen if we could not get around? Would we all get to work and to school, or would we all be stuck at home unable to get to the shops to buy food and all of the other things we need? That's a little bit like the situation in the brain of someone with ADHD. Sometimes there aren't enough neurotransmitters to make sure messages move from one part of the brain to the other. But maybe your brain isn't meant to use a car and bus transport system. Maybe it's meant to be different.

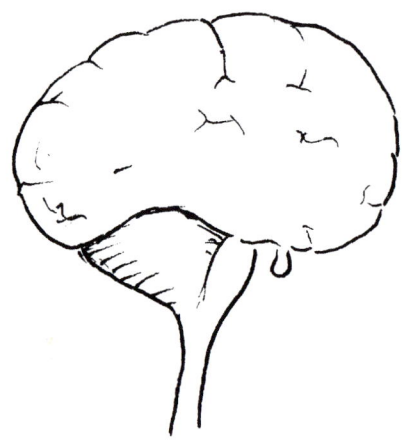

## ADHD has a purpose

If you have ADHD you may find it brings with it many advantages. People with ADHD are often good look-outs because they are so good at noticing everything that's going on around them. They make good emergency workers like paramedics.

ADHD tends to run in families. If you think of your relatives you might be able to recognise members of your family who are a bit like yourself.

Jot down any members of your family you think you may be like. You might want to discuss this with your parents, sometimes they can tell you about what they were like when they were young, or what their brothers and sisters were like.

1.


2.


3.


4.

## Food and drink

Food and drink affects everyone's behaviour, but if you have ADHD you need to be particularly careful about what you eat. Some people with ADHD have allergies or are sensitive to some foods and drinks. This results in them having less control of their behaviour when they have been eating or drinking them.

**Dodgy food and drink**

- tomatoes 
- oranges
- orange juice 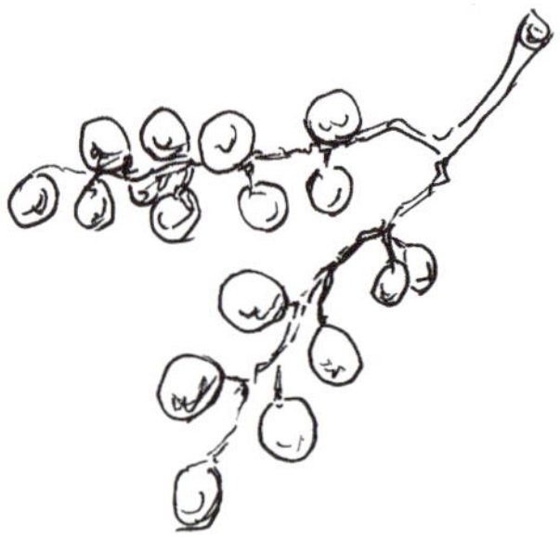
- fizzy drinks
- grapes 
- any foods with colourings or E numbers (sweets)
- sugary foods (chocolate)

"Oh no!" you're thinking those are some of my favourites. Your body can become addicted to these foods and you feel you can't do without them. Then when you have some you feel better – for a little while, until the bad behaviour starts.

SELF·ESTEEM

**What could you eat or drink instead?**

- 
- 
- 
- 

**Good Food & Drink**

- pasta
- bananas
- chicken
- potatoes
- most fresh fruit
- cheese
- yoghurt
- cereals
- water
  (this is the best drink)

**I like**

- 
- 
- 
- 
- 
- 
- 
- 
- 

SELF-ESTEEM

If you are taking tablets for your ADHD you might find they take away your appetite. Try to eat at the times you are hungry, such as when the medicine is wearing off late at night, and before you take your first tablet in the morning. A bowl of cereal at night can be a good idea.

Can you plan a menu? Remember which foods are good for you.

**Breakfast**


**Lunch**


**Dinner**


**Supper**


**Snacks**

Are there any foods in that list that might be giving you a bad reaction, or that contain a lot of sugar or E numbers? Have a look on labels to see what's in food before you eat it. Your body is very precious so look after it.

| Food | Ingredients |
| --- | --- |
| 1. Ice cream | |
| 2. Baked beans | |
| 3. Tomato ketchup | |

**SELF-ESTEEM**

## *About myself*

The trouble with having ADHD is that it can be very hard to concentrate on some things. Even though you may be a really intelligent person some people might call you a scatterbrain because you forget about things and lose things. This annoys other people and sometimes they can be really hurtful to you and make you feel bad about yourself when you feel you can't help it.

Help is here. You can do something to train your brain – but you have to want to do it.

Describe yourself by filling in these statements.

My name is _____ .

I am _____ years _____ months old.

I am _____ cm tall.

My eyes are _____ .

I am _____ kg in weight.

My hair is _____ .

I have _____ brothers and _____ sisters.

Their names are

_____

_____

_____ .

SELF-AWARENESS

I live with

_____

_____

_____

_____ .

I live at

_____

_____

_____ Postcode _____

Telephone number _____ .

Email address _____ .

This is me:

SELF-AWARENESS

## *Would you rather...*

- Have a bath in treacle OR mud?

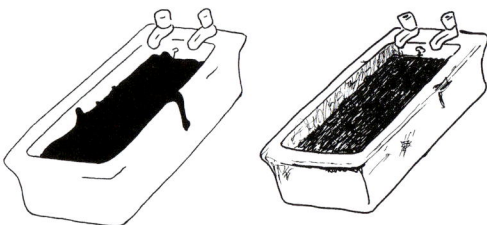

- Eat a plate of cabbage OR a bar of chocolate?

- Have a lesson where you move about and do things OR sit and write?

- Draw a picture OR do a page of handwriting?

- Listen to some music OR listen to someone talk?

- Tell jokes OR tell stories?

- Do some maths OR play football?

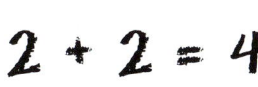

- Live in a hot country OR live in a cold country?

- Play chess OR ride your bike?

- Go swimming OR go to the pictures?

Try asking a friend the same questions or make up some of your own. See how much you have in common with your friend.

SELF-AWARENESS

## Your interview with a magazine journalist

Imagine news has got round that you are a very interesting person (because you are). A national magazine is sending their top journalist out to interview you. They are interested in finding out all about you and have sent a sheet of questions for you to think about before they see you.

What is your favourite game?




What is the best film you've ever seen?




What is the best book you've ever read?




What is your favourite music?

**SELF-AWARENESS**

What is your favourite TV programme?

What do you concentrate best on?

When you are in the classroom, where are you sitting when you get on best with your work?

Who are the people who understand you most?

Why do you think they understand you? What do they do to make you feel they understand you?

SELF-AWARENESS

**SELF-AWARENESS**

Do you like to do anything when you are trying to listen to people, for example doodle?

What helps you to remember instructions you are given?

What are you very good at?

What are your favourite subjects?

Have you got a least favourite subject?

Would you like to get better at anything?

What have you got better at lately?

Thank you for thinking about these questions. If there are any that you were not able to answer today keep them in the back of your mind and return to them when you have an answer.

SELF-AWARENESS

## Affirmations

It might sound silly, but telling yourself that you are good at things makes you get better at them. It's all about believing in yourself. Have a go.

Cut out these cards. Choose a different one each day and say it to yourself in front of the mirror each morning and in the evening before bed. Try to repeat it in your head throughout the day.

SELF-AWARENESS

| | |
|---|---|
| Every day I feel happier, healthier and calmer. | I am accurate and quick. |
| I am happy and good. | I am alert and a good listener. |
| I am confident. | I am still and peaceful. |

| | |
|---|---|
| I am helpful. | I am successful. |
| I am kind and considerate. | I am good and lovable. |
| I am polite and kind. | I am a good friend. |
| I am patient and careful. | I can laugh at myself. |
| I am persistent and determined. | I am organised and plan my time. |

SELF-AWARENESS

## *A perfect day*

My perfect day would begin with…

After breakfast I would…

At school I would go to my favourite lessons…

At lunchtime I would play with…

*A perfect day*

In the afternoon my class would...

When I got home I would...

For tea I would have...

Before bed I would...

SELF-AWARENESS

## I am good at

Now fill in these 'I am good at' statements.

1. I am good at *cleaning my shoes.*

2. I am good at

3. I am good at

4. I am good at

5. I am good at

6. I am good at

7. I am good at

8. I am good at

## I am good at

## *Friends*

Friends are important for all sorts of reasons. They can:

- help you out when you have a problem,
- share in a special moment,
- listen to your jokes,
- visit places with you, or
- think of good ideas with you.

Can you think of some other reasons for having a friend?

- 
- 
- 
- 
- 
- 

*Friends*

## *Making friends*

Having ADHD can make it difficult to make and keep friends. Friends may sometimes find your energy and enthusiasm just too much so they need to have a rest from you.

This doesn't mean they don't like you, only that they get tired more quickly than you. Sometimes they can say and do nasty things because they are tired, and sometimes they wish they hadn't said or done those things.

You can practise making friends. You need to think about things you like to do, and of someone you know who you would like to do these things with.

For example:

I like James, together we could climb trees.

Now you do it.

I like _____,

together we could _____.

I like _____,

together we could _____.

I like _____,

together we could _____.

I like _____,

together we could _____.

Are you able to spend time with the friends you have mentioned above?

If not, talk to an adult to get help in arranging a favourite activity.

FRIENDS

## *Being a good friend*

Being a good friend means being able to give and take, being able to take turns, and being able to laugh at yourself. This is very important.

A good sense of humour is important. Many people with ADHD have a very good sense of humour. They love to laugh, to make jokes and fool around, but sometimes in the wrong place and at the wrong time. Having a good sense of humour is one of the greatest personality gifts you can have. Being able to laugh at yourself is another great gift. If you can laugh when things are getting you down you will soon be feeling better.

Look back over the last week and try to think of a time when you were able to see the funny side of something you did. Maybe you did something you were a bit embarrassed about but you were able to laugh about it.

Write down or tell your friend or teacher what happened. Remember you are thinking about seeing the funny side of your own behaviour.

This is what Darren told his friend:

"Last week I had to play a duet on the clarinet in a concert my music teacher was putting on with her pupils. I had been practising and was quite good at home. When it was time to start I positioned my fingers and started to blow. My partner played well, but I started to squeak and lose my timing. I felt like the comedy act and couldn't wait to get off stage. At the time it was awful, but on the way home my mum, dad and I couldn't stop laughing at how funny it was."

## Other people's games

Sometimes you will need to play games chosen by someone else. Games usually require you to take turns and keep to some simple rules.

Try playing some games with a friend. Cards are great for this.

Can you think of other games you can play? (Here are some ideas – board games such as Snakes and Ladders or Scrabble, card games like Snap and Rummy, or dice games like Yahtzee.) Describe one to your friend. Remember to tell him the rules. Now play it together.

Rules are important so that everyone knows what is expected of them in the game. When you have learnt to take turns with one other person try playing with two or more people.

## *Making up your own games*

It can be fun to make up your own games, but before you start you all need to know the rules. If you don't everyone gets muddled and upset because they don't understand.

Think of a game you and some friends have made up. What were the rules?

1.


2.


3.


4.


Did you sort the rules out first before you started to play properly?

Sometimes people with ADHD get described as bossy by their friends. That's because there are so many ideas rushing round in your head all at the same time that they come out in a rush without you being able to persuade people that they are good ideas.

Try slowing down and saying one thing at a time.

## What do you like about your friends?

Think about your friends. What do you like about them?

- 
- 
- 
- 
- 
- 
- 

**FRIENDS**

## What makes a perfect friend?

Describe your perfect friend.

**What makes a perfect friend?**

FRIENDS

## Slowing down

Sometimes you might be rushing around too fast, what can happen when you do?

You might...

- fall over.

- forget to dress properly.

- drop things.

- not have time to think up good ideas.

- knock things over.

- leave your PE kit in the bedroom.

- rush out of the lesson before taking down your homework.

- not read instructions properly.

Can you think of any more?

- 

- 

-

## *Learning to slow down*

Have you got loads of ideas? Do you think that the rest of the world can't keep up with you? Are you afraid that if you don't blurt them all out now you'll forget them?

Try this:

Instead of blurting them all out scribble them down - write or draw - on a piece of paper. When I'm teaching I use my blackboard for this. At home I use my fridge door like a whiteboard, or my diary - everything goes in that.

Sometimes it's really hard to remember things we need to do. One easy way is to write a list.

Make a list in words or pictures of all the things you want to do today. Here's an example of mine:

1) Have a bath

2) Ring my friend Sunita

3) Clean the kitchen floor

## *My to do today list*

Now it's your turn.

My to do today list

1. _____

2. _____

3. _____

4. _____

5. _____

6. _____

Knowing what needs to be done is half the battle. What you need to do now is put them in order of priority. What is most important? Put that at the top of the list. Now decide *when* you are going to do all the things on your list. This is called scheduling.

Now you try:

---

My Schedule

1. _____ at _____

2. _____ at _____

3. _____ at _____

4. _____ at _____

---

**Things to carry over to tomorrow**

Sometimes things need to be carried over to the next day. If you write down what they are you are less likely to forget them.

---

My to do tomorrow list

1. _____

2. _____

3. _____

I write lists for everything, and sometimes I cheat a bit by putting something on the list I've already done! It helps me feel I'm making progress. I break things down into little bits too. For example if I had some work to do, say some English homework in 3 sections a, b and c, my list would be:

My to do today list

1. English homework : Part a

2. _____ : Part b

3. _____ : Part c

As soon as I'd done part 'a', I'd cross it off.

My to do today list

1. English homework : ~~Part a~~

2. _____ : Part b

3. _____ : Part c

There, that feels much better. Before long you are ready to cross off part b and part c too.

## Things you can do to help you concentrate

A few simple activities can really help your brain to work well.

Try this. Read out the letters of the alphabet, but each one has a coded instruction with it. So, when you read 'A', you must bend your knees. Practise going faster and slower – see the key.

| A<br>B | B<br>N | C<br>S | D<br>B |
|---|---|---|---|
| E<br>S | F<br>N | G<br>S | H<br>B |
| I<br>N | J<br>B | K<br>N | L<br>S |
| M<br>N | N<br>S | O<br>B | P<br>B |
| Q<br>S | R<br>N | S<br>B | T<br>N |
| U<br>S | V<br>N | W<br>S | XYZ<br>B |

**Key**

**B** = Bend your knees
**N** = Touch your nose
**S** = Stretch up with both arms

A few simple movements/actions can also help you concentrate.

**Brain Gym**

Cross crawl is a 'Brain Gym' exercise. 'Brain Gym' is like an aerobics class for your brain. It helps both sides of your brain to work together. Walk on the spot and bring up each knee in turn to touch your opposite elbow – very slowly.

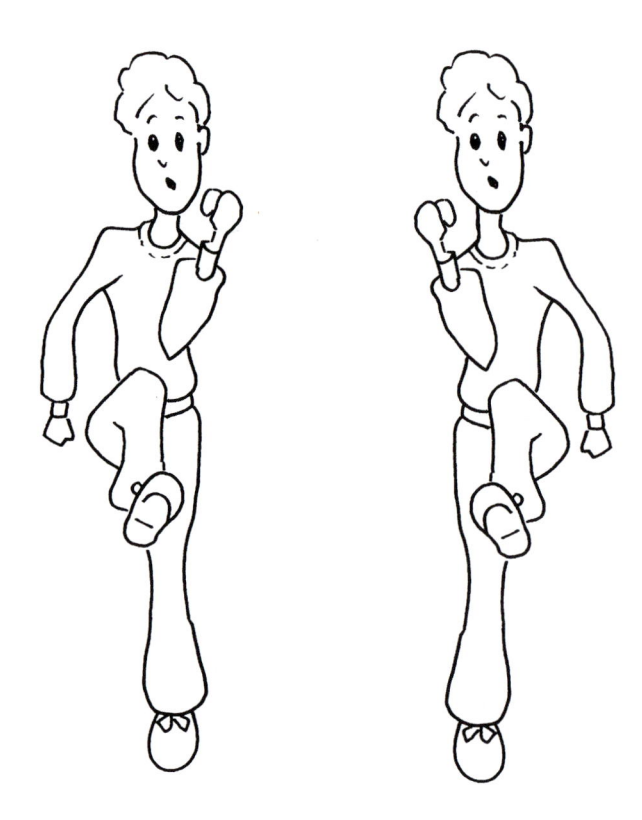

Do this ten times every morning and evening.

If you find this one too tricky touch each knee with the opposite hand instead.

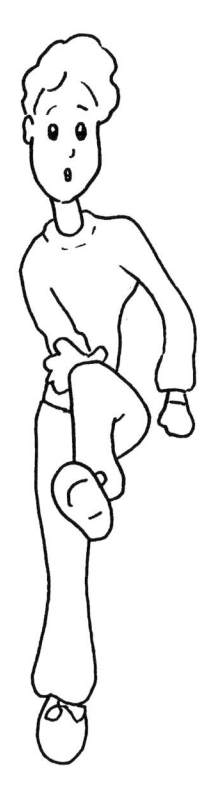

The important thing to remember here is that you must touch your right leg with your left hand or elbow, then cross over to touch your left leg with your right hand.

There are lots more 'Brain Gym' exercises in a book called *Smart Moves* by Carla Hannaford.

Now try this activity.

Start like this:

**A**

then...

**B** Hold your nose with your right hand. Hold your right ear with your left hand.

now...

**C** Hold your nose with your left hand. Hold your left ear with your right hand.

Now practice the five times table. When the answer is even – go into position B. For odd numbers change to position C – go as fast as you can. Now practice the seven times table.

| | | | |
|---|---|---|---|
| 1 x 5 = 5 | 6 x 5 = 30 | 1 x 7 = 7 | 6 x 7 = 42 |
| 2 x 5 = 10 | 7 x 5 = 35 | 2 x 7 = 14 | 7 x 7 = 49 |
| 3 x 5 = 15 | 8 x 5 = 40 | 3 x 7 = 21 | 8 x 7 = 56 |
| 4 x 5 = 20 | 9 x 5 = 45 | 4 x 7 = 28 | 9 x 7 = 63 |
| 5 x 5 = 25 | 10 x 5 = 50 | 5 x 7 = 35 | 10 x 7 = 70 |

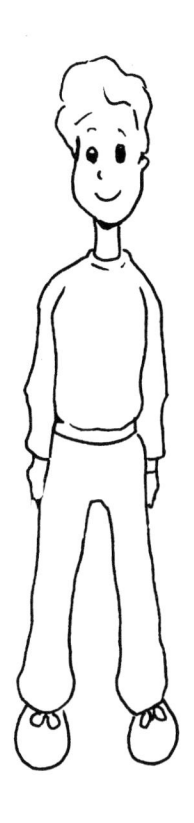

**Yoga**

This is a yoga posture. Yoga is really good for helping you to concentrate.

It is called 'Tadasana', which means 'the mountain'.

1. Stand with your feet hip width apart and heels and toes parallel.

2. Roll your shoulders gently to relax them.

3. Let your arms hang loosely by your sides.

4. Imagine there is a piece of string attached to the top of your head and it is gently pulling you up, gently stretching out your back bone. You should be a little taller now.

5. Keep your shoulders back and relaxed, with your arms hanging by your sides.

6. Now try to stand still for a few seconds, close your eyes if you can.

This can be very relaxing.

For lots more yoga look at a book called *Yoga for Children* by Mary Stewart and Kathy Phillips.

### Making your own relaxation tape

You can make your own relaxation tape to help you relax when you are feeling tense. Read the script below slowly into the microphone on your tape recorder.

You will need:

- A tape recorder
- A tape
- This script
- A quiet place
- Some of your favourite relaxing music

### Script

Sit comfortably in the chair.
Make sure both feet are flat on the floor.
Make sure your bottom is well back on the seat of the chair.
Make sure your back is straight.
Check you are looking straight ahead of you.
Now close your eyes.

Place one hand on your chest and one on your tummy.
Take three slow breaths.

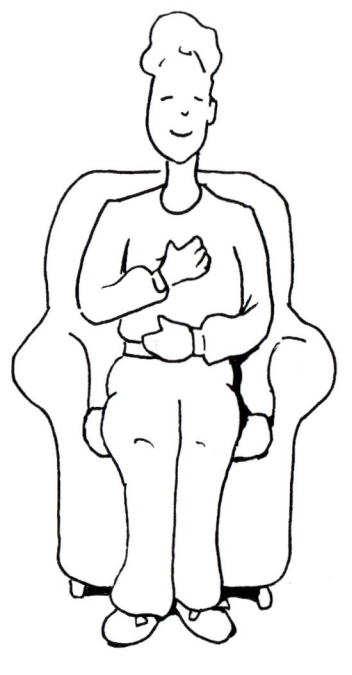

In ... out
In ... out
In ... out

Check which hand is moving the most.
Put the other hand back in your lap.
Take three more slow breaths.

In ... out
In ... out
In ... out

Place the other hand in your lap.
Keep your breathing slow.

Think about your toes.
Scrunch them up tight as you breathe in.
Hold for a breath out and in.
Let them relax on your next out breath.

Think about your legs.
Tighten the muscles in your legs as you breathe in.
Hold for a breath out and in.
Let them relax on your next out breath.

Think about the muscles around the base of your spine.
Tighten those muscles.
Hold for a breath out and in.
Let them relax on your next out breath.

Think about your chest and upper back.
Tighten those muscles.
Hold for a breath out and in.
Let them relax on your next out breath.

Think about your arms and hands.
Tighten those muscles, make fists with your hands.
Hold for a breath out and in.
Let them relax on your next out breath.

Think about your neck and face.
Tighten those muscles, make a really ugly face, stick your tongue right out.
Hold for a breath out and in.
Let them relax on your next out breath.

Now you have worked right through your body, you can tell the difference between tense and relaxed.

Scan your whole body to check for tense parts and relax them down as you breathe out.

Let go of tensions and thoughts.

Breathe slowly for five breaths trying to stay relaxed.

In ... out
In ... out
In ... out
In ... out
In ... out

Rub your hands together.
Place them over your eyes.
Open your fingers slightly.
Open your eyes.
Gradually open your fingers a little more.
Slide your hands down your cheeks bringing them to rest in your lap.

How do you feel?

You might like to add some of your favourite relaxing music at the end of this tape.

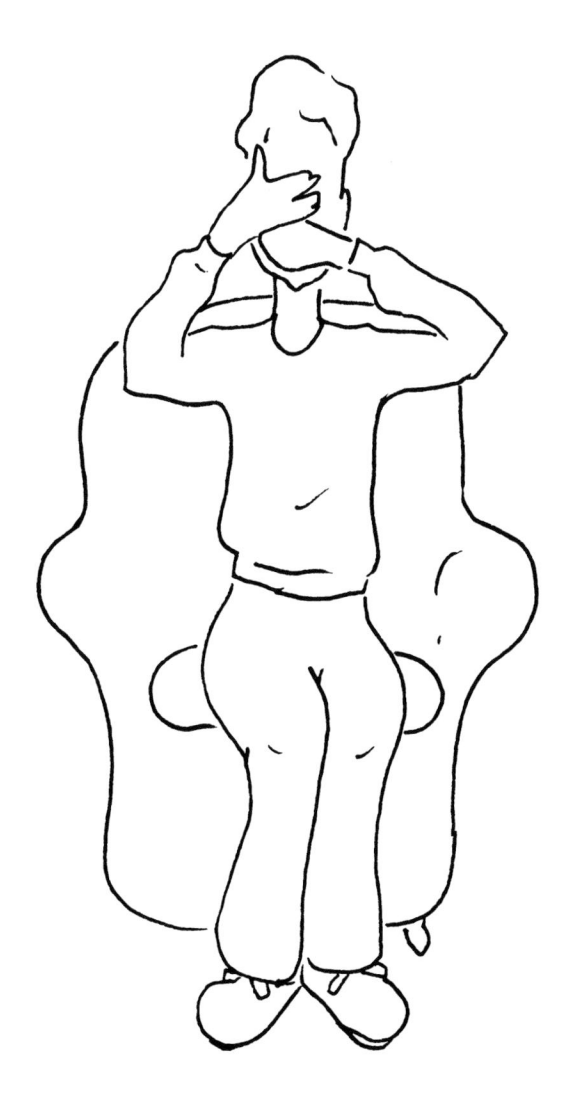

## Puzzles

Puzzles like 'spot the difference' can help you to slow down and concentrate on your work. Try finding the nine differences in the puzzles below.

It's good to practise this kind of exercise. See if you can find any more books with puzzles like this in. There are usually a few at the local newsagents.

### Sequencing

Sometimes you might want to do so many things all at the same time that you get confused as to what order to do them in. Knowing what order to do things in is called sequencing. If you are the type of person who only thinks about putting a raincoat on after you are soaked, maybe you should practise sequencing.

Put these pictures in order by writing the numbers 1–4 in the boxes below them.

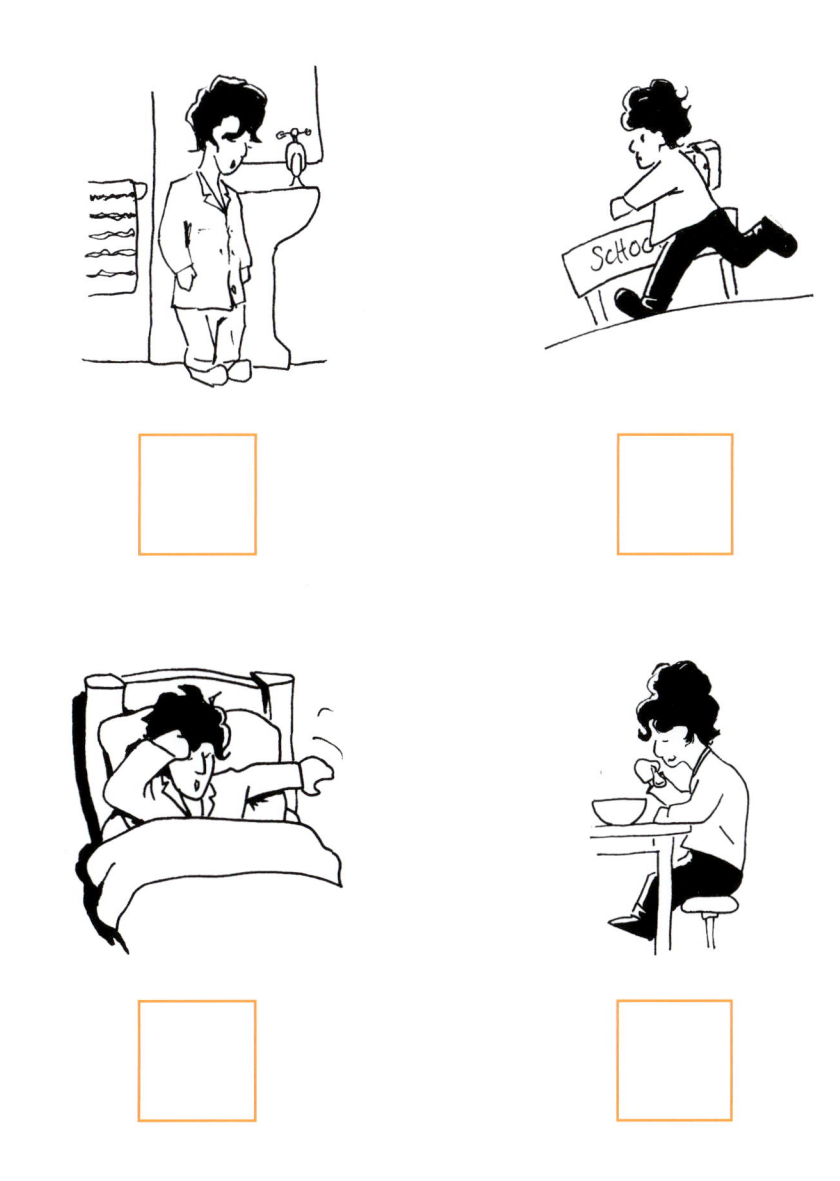

Need a harder one? Ask your teacher.

## Following instructions

It is important to read all the instructions before you start.

Follow the instructions below.

---

1. Write your name at the top of this box.
2. Underline your name in pencil.
3. Draw a picture of a man and/or woman in space a).

a)



4. Complete only instruction 1 in this box.

---

Did you follow all of the instructions? It is important to read all the instructions first.

### *Writing your own instructions*

Can you write a set of instructions for making beans on toast?

Or a set of directions between your classroom and the library?

- 
- 
- 
- 

Ask your friend to follow the instructions. Did they work?

## Circle pictures

Now try this.

Making pictures and patterns inside a circle is a very calming thing to do. It will help your thoughts to come in a more ordered way.

In the circles, fill in your own patterns or pictures.

63

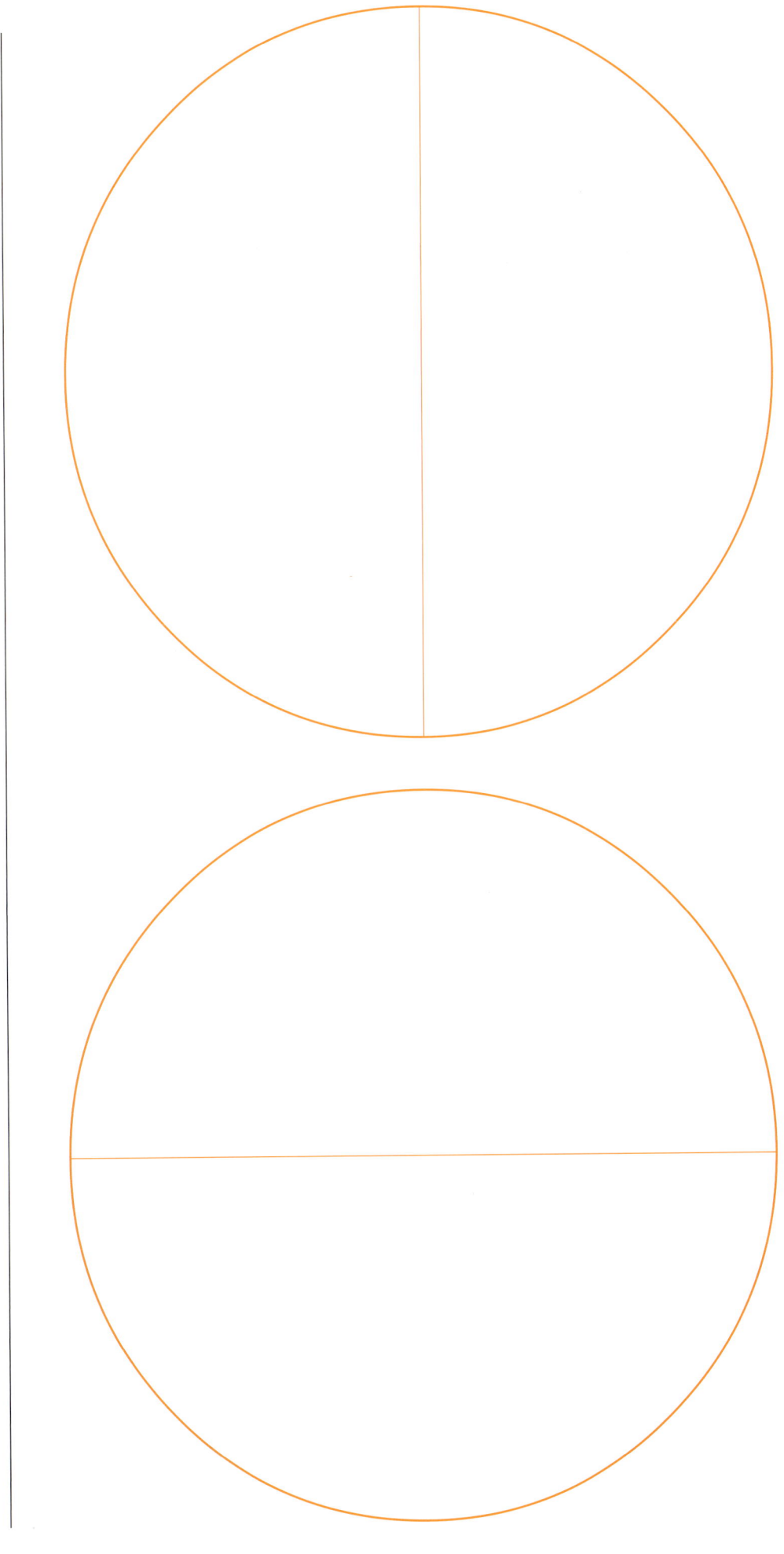

SUPPORTING CHILDREN

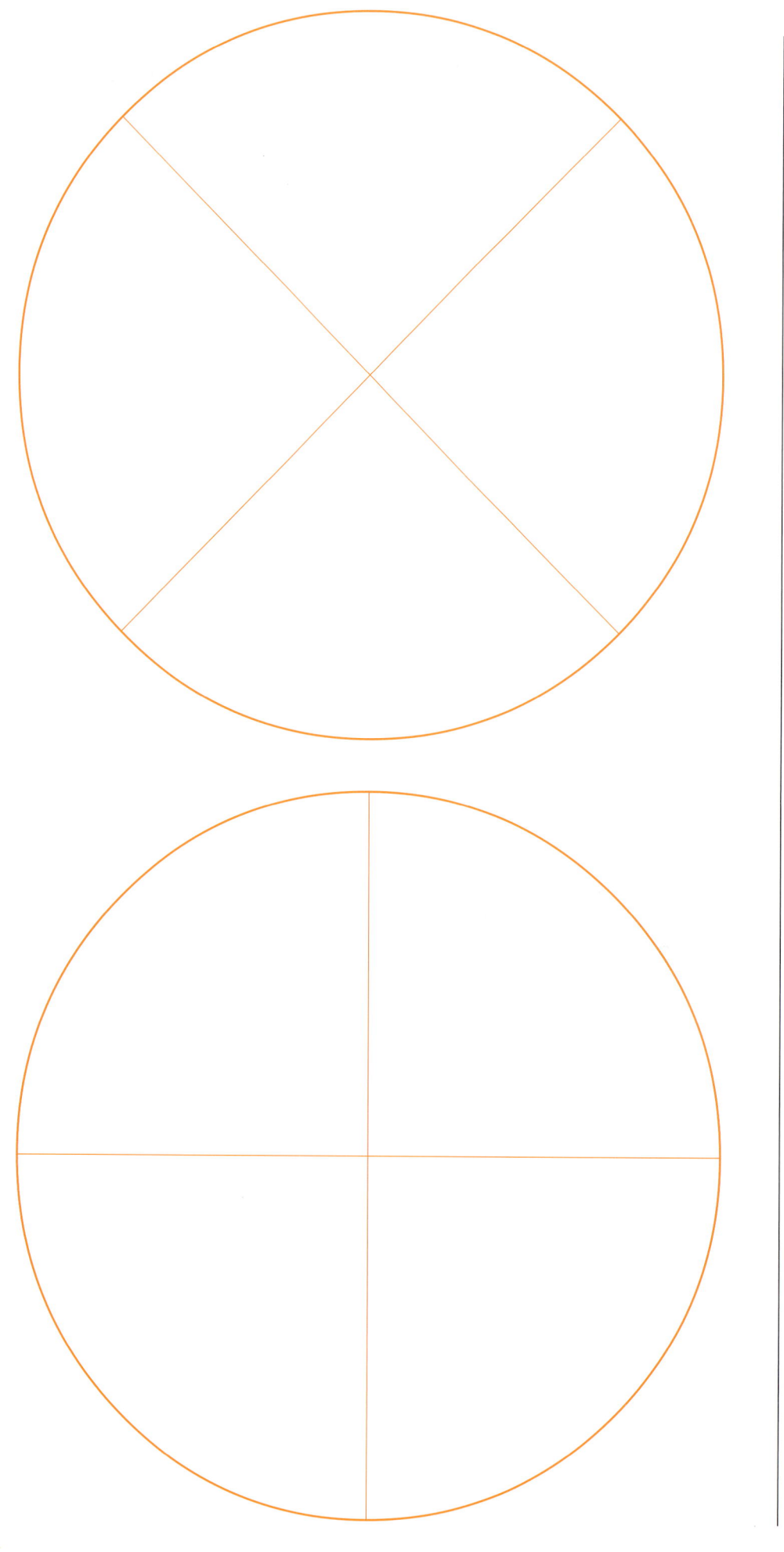

**64**

SUPPORTING CHILDREN

ORGANISATION & CONCENTRATION

Here are some ideas of patterns you can make using compasses.

## Time management

**Here are some hints on how to manage your time well**

1. Slow down and work carefully.

2. Break jobs down into small parts.

3. Make a plan of how you are going to get the parts done.

4. Work with other people – it can be more fun and make the work easier.

**How long will it take?**

Sometimes when we plan we make mistakes in guessing how long it will take to do something. If you have some homework to do as well as all the other things you want to do in an evening, you need to work out how long each thing is likely to take. This will help you plan to do everything that you need to.

Write down how long you think it will take to do the following things. Then time yourself, or get someone else to time you doing them.

|  | Guess | Actual time |
|---|---|---|
| Have a bath or shower |  |  |
| Eat my tea |  |  |
| Complete my homework |  |  |

How did you do? Were your guesses close to the actual time, or were they a bit out? If they were too short, you know that you need to allow yourself more time to get things done. If they were too long you know you can try to do more things than you are doing.

BUT be careful. Try to make sure that whatever you do, you do well.

Keep practising this – you will become good at knowing what you do and don't have time for.

## Planning assignments

As you get older you will have larger pieces of work to do like assignments. I find a good way to start these assignments is by 'Brainstorming'.

Say the assignment is on the Ancient Greeks, here's what I would do.

1. Write the assignment title in the middle of the page
2. All around, anywhere you like, write down in pictures or words, thoughts and questions connected with the Ancient Greeks.

The idea is to sweep out your brain of anything you can think of to do with the assignment. That way you won't forget your good ideas because you will have a note of them and you can get them organised into some kind of order. You can do this by using a tape recorder, try speaking your ideas and questions onto a tape. The main thing is that you have a record of them for later.

## Ancient Greeks: Brainstorming sheet

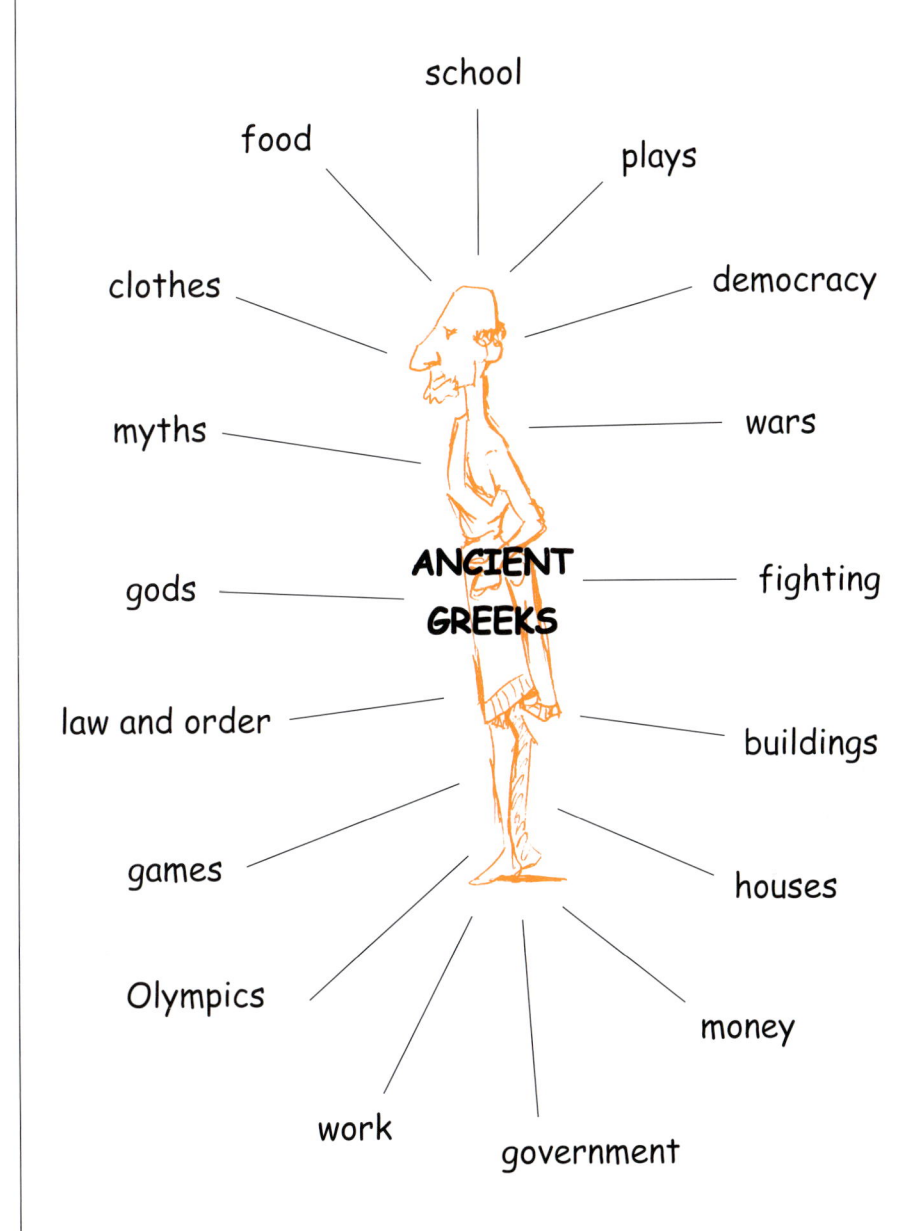

- school
- food
- plays
- clothes
- democracy
- myths
- wars
- gods
- **ANCIENT GREEKS**
- fighting
- law and order
- buildings
- games
- houses
- Olympics
- money
- work
- government

By doing this you think of ideas and questions that you can find out more about.

## Brainstorming sheet

Use this sheet to brainstorm ideas for your own topic. Remember to write the topic title in the middle of the page.

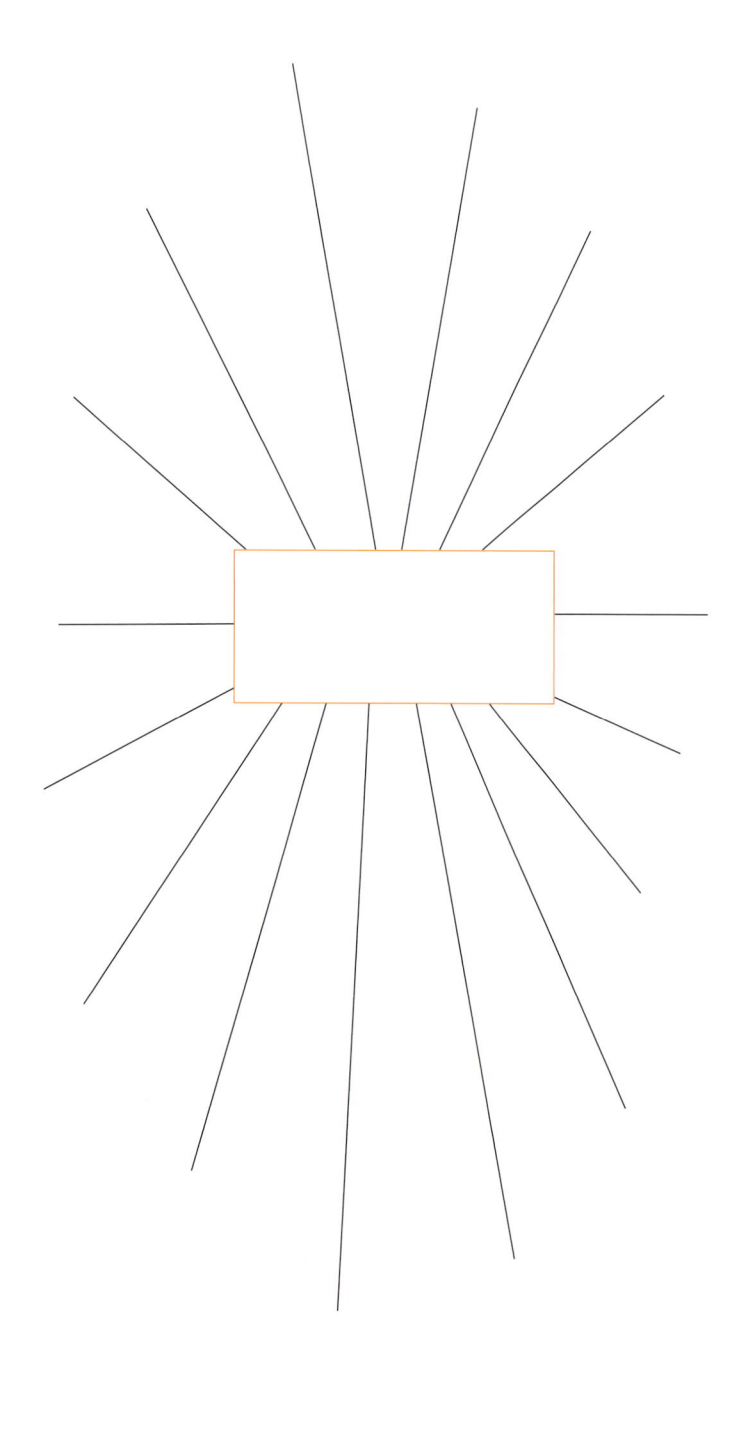

## Drawing up a plan of action

Now that you have done your first bit of thinking, and you have kept a note of your ideas, you need to plan when and how you are going to do the 'finding out'. This is where the work you did earlier, trying to guess the length of time it will take to do something, will come in really handy.

Here is an example of a plan of action:

|      | Lesson time | Lunch time | After school |
|------|-------------|------------|--------------|
| Mon  | Brainstorm. Decide on questions to be answered. | | Surf the Net for info. |
| Tues | | School library. | |
| Wed  | | | Town library. |
| Thur | Discuss what you have found with your teacher and friends. | Decide which bits you want to use. | Discuss what you have found with your parents. |
| Fri  | Get drawing, writing, tape recording, videoing and word processing. Remember you also have the weekend to work on your assignment. Completed and handed in on Monday. | | |

This assignment plan is for a short assignment lasting only one week. Now choose a topic and draw up your own plan of action.

|  | Mon | Tues | Wed | Thur | Fri and the weekend |
|---|---|---|---|---|---|
| Lesson time |  |  |  |  |  |
| Lunch time |  |  |  |  |  |
| After school |  |  |  |  |  |

Once you understand how to draw up a plan of action for a short assignment you can try planning longer ones. When you do have a bigger assignment to do, you need to 'chunk' it. This means you split it into bits you can cope with.

Think of an assignment as your favourite treat. My favourite treat is a chocolate bar. Imagine the biggest size they do. If you tried to stick it all in your mouth in one go you wouldn't be able to chew it to eat it. So you need to bite off a chunk you can get in your mouth. If you do that it tastes really good. A big chocolate bar takes a few bites to eat comfortably. Sometimes you need a bit of a break in between chunks, you can feel a bit sick if you eat too much too quickly.

Eating a big chocolate bar is just like doing an assignment – take it in chunks and you will enjoy the experience, try to do it in one go and you could end up feeling sick.

## Evening plan

Plans come in handy for other things too. To make sure you have time to fit everything into your hectic life make a plan for the evening.

| 3:30 | Arrive home – healthy snack |
|---|---|
| 4:00 | Homework |
| 4:30 | Free time – TV, Playstation |
| 5:15 | Homework |
| 5:45 | Dinner |
| 6:15 | Jobs – washing up, tidy room |
| 7:00 | Practice music |
| 7:20 | Play with friends |
| 8:30 | Bath |
| 9:00 | Exercise – relaxation |
| 9:20 | Bed – reading and affirmation for the day |

Now you try...

My plan for _____ (day of the week)

|  | |
|---|---|
| 3:30 | |
| 4:00 | |
| 4:30 | |
| 5:00 | |
| 5:30 | |
| 6:00 | |
| 6:30 | |
| 7:00 | |
| 7:30 | |
| 8:00 | |
| 8:30 | |
| 9:00 | |
| 9:30 | |
| 10:00 | |

Is your plan the same for every day of the week, or do you need to make different plans for other days?

## What learning and working style suits you?

Some people learn and work best listening to music. Some work best early in the morning, others late at night. If you know how you learn and work well you can use that knowledge to help you get your work done. You would be amazed at the difference it makes to work in conditions and at a time that suits your mind and body.

For each of the statements below choose a number from 1-4 and write it in the box.

**1**　　　　　**2**　　　　　**3**　　　　　**4**
Disagree　　　　　　　　　　　　　　　Agree

Say to yourself 'I learn and work best when…'

- [ ] I have just got up
- [ ] I've just had my lunch
- [ ] I've just had my tea
- [ ] Just before I go to bed
- [ ] I'm on my own
- [ ] I'm with friends
- [ ] I'm with an adult
- [ ] It's quiet
- [ ] There is relaxing music
- [ ] There is a lot of noise
- [ ] I'm lying down
- [ ] I'm sitting at my desk alone
- [ ] I'm sitting at a table with lots of other people
- [ ] I can get up and walk around when I want to
- [ ] I can write things down

- [ ] I can draw pictures as answers to questions
- [ ] I can read out loud
- [ ] I can hear instructions
- [ ] I can read instructions
- [ ] I can be shown instructions
- [ ] I have someone who can test me on my work
- [ ] I am sitting on a comfortable chair
- [ ] I am warm
- [ ] The light in the room is bright
- [ ] I don't want to go to the toilet
- [ ] I have had a recent snack
- [ ] I have had a recent drink of water
- [ ] I can get up and stretch
- [ ] I can make noises and talk to myself

The last two might sound a bit crazy, but if you watch people while they are thinking hard they do some funny things. The only snag is that while making noises might be great for the person making them they can be very distracting for everyone else in the room. Some things are best kept for homework!

You need to discuss these last two pages with your teacher and parent or carer so that they know how you work best and can help you.

Remember knowing when and how you work best is not an excuse not to work under any other conditions. It does mean you can help yourself, and others around you can help and encourage you to work when it suits you best.

GOOD LUCK!

## *A few final tips*

- Start the day with cross crawl ten times and an affirmation.

- When doing something that requires a lot of sitting still and concentrating break it up with something to refresh your concentration like cross crawl or a little circle picture.

- Always remember you are better at a lot of things than many other people.

- Use your energy in a positive way.

- Learn how to relax and use the technique often.

- Remember some days will be better than others.

- Even when you don't feel great, there are still a lot of great things about you.

## *Congratulations*

Congratulations, you have reached the last page!

I hope some of the things you have done on your journey through this book will have helped you to develop some good work routines so that life becomes easier for you, and so that people can see just how capable you are when you can keep your mind on things.

Remember if you know how your brain works, and by now you should have some idea about how you work best, you can work in ways that suit you. BUT you will have to make sure you discuss these things with your teachers and parents or carers, because they need to know how they can help you to do your best.

Good luck, and don't forget to let me know how you got on.

Email: spohrer@hotmail.com

## Further reading

Anderson R (1999), *First Steps to a Physical Basis of Concentration*, Crown House Publishing, Carmarthen, UK.

Buzan T (1999), *The Mindmap Book*, BBC Books, London, UK.

Hannaford C (1995), *Smart Moves*, Great Ocean Publishers, Virginia, USA.

Hartmann T (1999), *Attention Deficit Disorder, A Different Perception*, Newleaf, Dublin, Eire.

Holowenko H (1999), *Attention Deficit/Hyperactivity Disorder, A Multidisciplinary Approach*, Jessica Kingsley, London, UK.

Hyperactive Children's Support Group (2001), *Hyperactivity in the Classroom – A brief guide for teachers and parents*, HACSG, 71 Whyke Lane, Chichester, West Sussex PO19 2LD, UK.

Munden A, Arcelus J (1999), *The ADHD Handbook*, Jessica Kingsley, London, UK.

Nicholson-Nelson K (1998), *Developing Students' Multiple Intelligences*, Scholastic, New York, USA.

Smith A, Call N (1999), *The ALPS Approach – Accelerated Learning in Primary Schools*, Network Educational Press, Stafford, UK.

Stewart M, Phillips K (1992), *Yoga for Children*, Vermillion, London, UK.

# Special Children

# Supporting Children Series

The *Supporting Children* books are aimed at educational practitioners, both teachers and learning assistants, in specialist and non-specialist settings. Each book provides theory to inform the reader about a specific special need, while the main body of the text offers practical advice, support and activities to facilitate pupils' learning.

### Coming soon:

**Supporting Children with Dyslexia**

A guide to dyslexia with a balance of information and practical ideas for use with pupils who have this condition.

## Supporting Children with Multiple Disabilities

By following the practical framework provided, teachers will be able to implement a multi-sensory curriculum in the classroom. This will enable children with multiple disabilities to become more independent and active, and to develop effective communication skills.

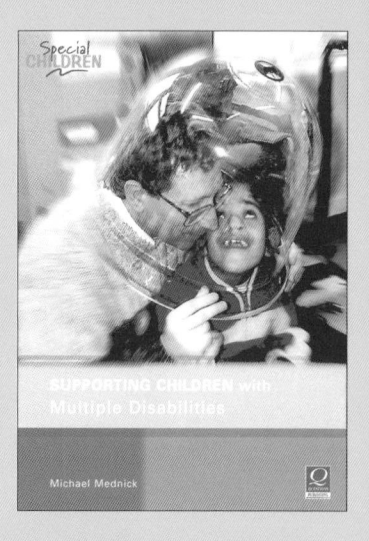

**Price:** £14.99   **ISBN:** 1-84190-042-7   **Format:** A4 Approx. 180pp

## Supporting Children with Autism in Mainstream Schools

It is increasingly common for children with autism to attend mainstream schools. Using the child-centred, whole-school approach provided in this resource, teachers will be able to implement strategies for supporting these children in the classroom, and successfully meeting their learning needs.

**Price:** £14.99   **ISBN:** 1-84190-055-9   **Format:** A4 Approx. 80pp

## Supporting Children with Speech and Language Impairment and Associated Difficulties

How do you identify pupils with speech and language impairment? This guide outlines the main areas of difficulty for pupils, and suggests how teachers can make the curriculum more accessible and so facilitate greater learning.

**Price:** £14.99   **ISBN:** 1-84190-083-4   **Format:** A4 Approx. 128pp

# Order form

I wish to place an order for the following titles:

Supporting Children with Multiple Disabilities
£14.99 each
☐ copies

Supporting Children with Autism in Mainstream Schools
£14.99 each
☐ copies

Supporting Children with Speech and Language Impairment and Associated Difficulties
£14.99 each
☐ copies

PLEASE SEND MY ORDER TO:

Name: _____

Job title: _____

Delivery address: _____

_____

Postcode: _____

Tel: _____ Fax: _____

Email: _____

For Postage and Packing add: £3.00 UK – £5.00 Overseas

☐ I enclose a cheque for £_____

made payable to The Questions Publishing Company Ltd.

☐ I wish to pay by credit card:

No. ☐☐☐☐ ☐☐☐☐ ☐☐☐☐ ☐☐☐☐ ☐☐☐☐

Expiry date: ☐☐☐☐

Please give card address if different from delivery address:

_____

Postcode: _____ Tel: _____

☐ I wish to pay by Official Order no. _____

**Credit Card Hotline
0121 666 7878**

Fax orders 0121 666 7879
Email sales@questpub.co.uk

Return completed form to
The Questions Publishing Company Ltd,
1st Floor, Leonard House,
321 Bradford Street,
Digbeth, Birmingham B5 6ET